CONTINENTS

AUSTRALIA
AND
OCEANIA

Kate Darian-Smith

WAYLAND

CONTINENTS

AFRICA

ANTARCTICA

ASIA

AUSTRALIA AND
OCEANIA

EUROPE

NORTH AMERICA

SOUTH AMERICA

First published in 1996 by
Wayland (Publishers) Limited
61 Western Road, Hove
East Sussex, BN3 1JD, England
© Copyright 1996 Wayland (Publishers) Limited

Australian Picture Library 16, 23, 28, 30, 31, 32; Camerapress 21,
39; Frank Spencer 29; Hutchison Library 13, 20, 40; Impact 17, 24,
35, 38, 41, 43; New Zealand Tourist Board 25; Science Photo Library
10, 15; Trip 11, 13, 20, 22, 27, 30, 31, 33, 34, 36, 37; Zefa 18, 19,
35, 42, 43

Produced for Wayland (Publishers) Limited
by *specialist* publishing services, London
Designer: Mark Whitchurch

British Library Cataloguing in Publication Data
Australia and Oceania - (Continents)
1 Australia - Juvenile Literature 2 Oceania - Juvenile
Literature
I. Title
994'.063

ISBN 0 7502 1500 3

Typeset by Mark Whitchurch Art & Design, England
Maps by Peter Bull
Graph artwork by Mark Whitchurch
Printed and bound in Italy by G. Canale

CONTENTS

AUSTRALIA AND OCEANIA BY COUNTRY

AUSTRALIA

Australia is a continent in its own right, and in terms of land area (7,682,300 km²) is the sixth-largest country in the world. It is the dominant political and economic power in the Pacific region. Australia is a significant middle-level power by international standards, with trade and foreign relations oriented towards other countries in the Asia-Pacific area. The nation has rich natural resources and a range of many different environments. Australia has a developed, industrial economy, but it is also a significant agricultural producer of wool, beef and wheat. The Australian population of 17.6 million enjoy a high standard of living. These are some of the factors that distinguish Australia from the smaller countries of Oceania.

PAPUA NEW GUINEA
Capital: Port Moresby
Area: 462,840 km²
Population: 3.6 million, 84 per cent rural
Currency: Kina
GNP per person ($): 1120
Principal languages: English, Pidgin, and hundreds of Melanesian principal languages.

Port Moresby

Darwin

NORTHERN TERRITORY

WESTERN AUSTRALIA

QUEENSLAND

Brisbane

SOUTH AUSTRALIA

NEW SOUTH WALES

Sydney

Perth

Adelaide

Canberra

Melbourne

VICTORIA

AUSTRALIA
Capital: Canberra
Area: 7,682,300 km²
Population: 17.6 million, 85 per cent urban
Currency: Australian dollar (A$)
GNP per person ($): 17510
Principal languages: English.

| 0 | 200 | 400 | 600 | 800 | 1000 km |
| 0 | 100 | 200 | 300 | 400 | 500 | 600 miles |

Hobart

MELANESIA

Melanesia is one of three main island groups of Oceania. The term Melanesia comes from the two Greek words meaning 'black islands', because of the dark-skinned peoples living in the region. The islands of Melanesia cover a vast area covering millions of square kilometres of land and sea to the north and east of Australia and to the south of the equator.

This is a region of great contrast between the different cultures spread throughout the islands. New Guinea is the largest Melanesian island, and the second-largest island in the world. Other Melanesian countries include the Solomon Islands, Vanuatu, and Fiji.

SOLOMON ISLANDS

Capital: Honiara, on Guadalcanal Island
Area: 28,370 km²
Population: 350,000
Currency: Solomon Islands dollar
GNP per person ($): 750
Principal languages: English and over 100 Melanesian principal languages.

Honiara

0	200	400	600	800 km
0	100	200	300	400	500 miles

VANUATU

Capital: Port Vila, on Éfaté Island
Area: 12,190 km²
Population: 154,000
Currency: Vatu
GNP per person ($): 1230
Principal languages: more than 100 Melanesian principal languages, Bislama, English, French.

Port Vila

Suva

FIJI

Capital: Suva, on Viti Levu
Area: 18,376 km²
Population: 760,000, 43 per cent urban
Currency: Fiji dollar
GNP per person ($): 2140
Principal languages: English, Fijian, Hindustani.

Noumea

NEW CALEDONIA

Capital: Nouméa
Area: 19,103 km²
Population: 169,900, 50 per cent live on Nouméa
Currency: Pacific French franc
GNP per person ($): 6000
Principal languages: 30 Melanesian principal languages, French.

MICRONESIA

Micronesia, which means 'tiny islands', is located to the north of Melanesia. This island group is situated in the west Pacific Ocean, and contains about 2,000 islands. Most of these islands are low-lying, and are made from coral. They include Guam, the Mariana Islands, the Marshall Islands, Nauru and Kiribati.

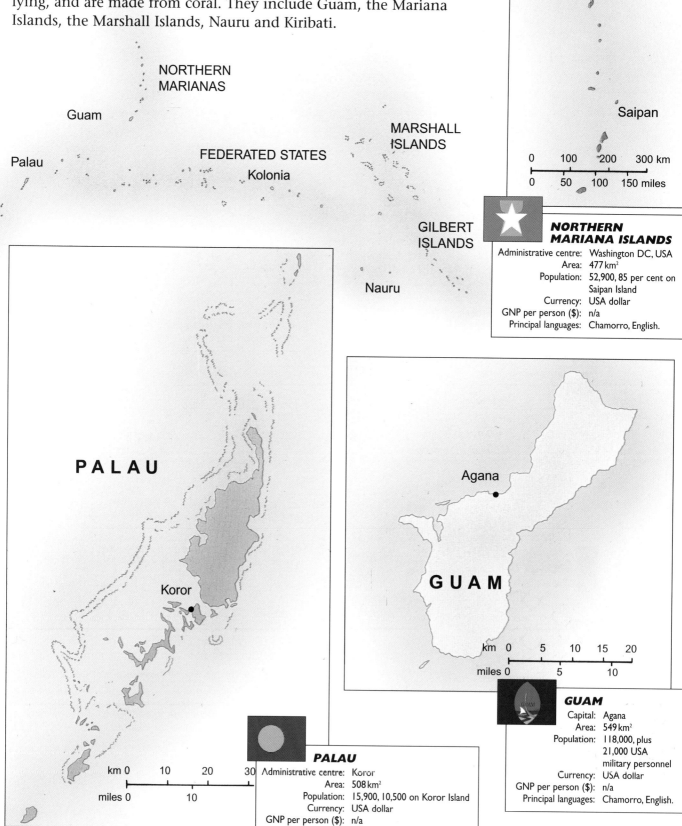

NORTHERN
MARIANAS

Guam

Palau

FEDERATED STATES

Kolonia

NORTHERN
MARIANAS

Saipan

| 0 | 100 | 200 | 300 km |
| 0 | 50 | 100 | 150 miles |

MARSHALL
ISLANDS

GILBERT
ISLANDS

Nauru

NORTHERN MARIANA ISLANDS

Administrative centre: Washington DC, USA
Area: 477 km²
Population: 52,900, 85 per cent on Saipan Island
Currency: USA dollar
GNP per person ($): n/a
Principal languages: Chamorro, English.

PALAU

Koror

| km 0 | 10 | 20 | 30 |
| miles 0 | 10 | |

PALAU

Administrative centre: Koror
Area: 508 km²
Population: 15,900, 10,500 on Koror Island
Currency: USA dollar
GNP per person ($): n/a
Principal languages: Palaun, English, Japanese.

Agana

GUAM

| km 0 | 5 | 10 | 15 | 20 |
| miles 0 | 5 | 10 | |

GUAM

Capital: Agana
Area: 549 km²
Population: 118,000, plus 21,000 USA military personnel
Currency: USA dollar
GNP per person ($): n/a
Principal languages: Chamorro, English.

Many of the islands of Micronesia (and Polynesia, see pages 8-9) are former colonies of European and American countries, and continue to be linked with them. Palau, the Marshall Islands and the Northern Marianas are linked to the USA; The Cook Islands and Tokelau are linked to New Zealand. Examining a country's currency is often a good way of guessing which other country it is linked with.

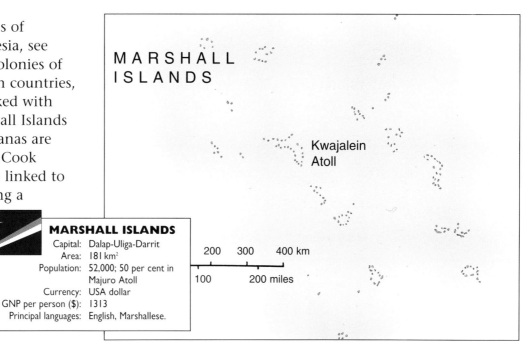

MARSHALL ISLANDS

Capital:	Dalap-Uliga-Darrit
Area:	181 km²
Population:	52,000; 50 per cent in Majuro Atoll
Currency:	USA dollar
GNP per person ($):	1313
Principal languages:	English, Marshallese.

FEDERATED STATES

YAP ISLANDS

TRUK ISLANDS

Ponape

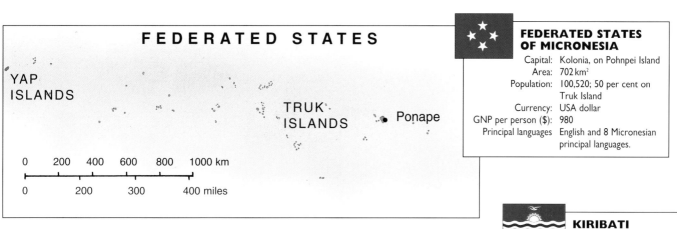

FEDERATED STATES OF MICRONESIA

Capital:	Kolonia, on Pohnpei Island
Area:	702 km²
Population:	100,520; 50 per cent on Truk Island
Currency:	USA dollar
GNP per person ($):	980
Principal languages	English and 8 Micronesian principal languages.

KIRIBATI

Capital:	Tarawa atoll
Area:	810 km²
Population:	73,000
Currency:	Australian dollar
GNP per person ($):	710
Principal languages:	English, Gilbertese.

NAURU

Yaren

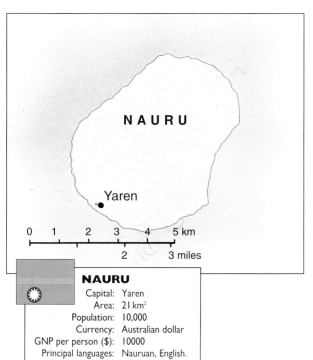

NAURU

Capital:	Yaren
Area:	21 km²
Population:	10,000
Currency:	Australian dollar
GNP per person ($):	10000
Principal languages:	Nauruan, English.

Tarawa Atoll

GILBERT ISLANDS

KIRIBATI

PHOENIX ISLANDS

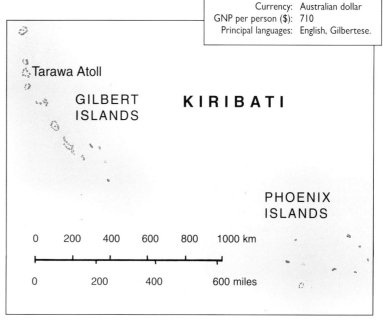

POLYNESIA

Polynesia, which means 'many islands', occupies a very large area in the eastern Pacific Ocean, and south of the equator. The large islands are generally volcanic and the smaller ones are made from coral. There are great distances between the islands. However, despite these distances the peoples of different Polynesian nations do share many similar cultural practices.

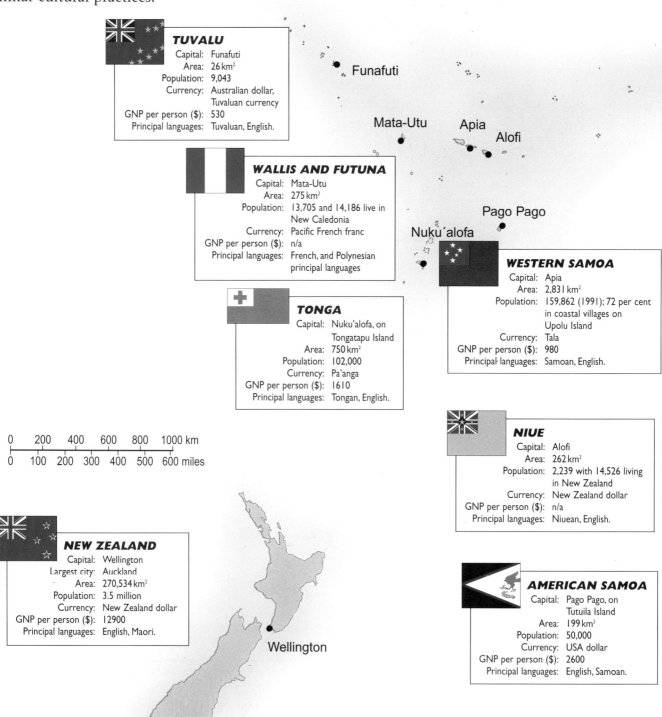

TUVALU
Capital: Funafuti
Area: 26 km²
Population: 9,043
Currency: Australian dollar, Tuvaluan currency
GNP per person ($): 530
Principal languages: Tuvaluan, English.

WALLIS AND FUTUNA
Capital: Mata-Utu
Area: 275 km²
Population: 13,705 and 14,186 live in New Caledonia
Currency: Pacific French franc
GNP per person ($): n/a
Principal languages: French, and Polynesian principal languages

TONGA
Capital: Nuku'alofa, on Tongatapu Island
Area: 750 km²
Population: 102,000
Currency: Pa'anga
GNP per person ($): 1610
Principal languages: Tongan, English.

WESTERN SAMOA
Capital: Apia
Area: 2,831 km²
Population: 159,862 (1991); 72 per cent in coastal villages on Upolu Island
Currency: Tala
GNP per person ($): 980
Principal languages: Samoan, English.

NIUE
Capital: Alofi
Area: 262 km²
Population: 2,239 with 14,526 living in New Zealand
Currency: New Zealand dollar
GNP per person ($): n/a
Principal languages: Niuean, English.

NEW ZEALAND
Capital: Wellington
Largest city: Auckland
Area: 270,534 km²
Population: 3.5 million
Currency: New Zealand dollar
GNP per person ($): 12900
Principal languages: English, Maori.

AMERICAN SAMOA
Capital: Pago Pago, on Tutuila Island
Area: 199 km²
Population: 50,000
Currency: USA dollar
GNP per person ($): 2600
Principal languages: English, Samoan.

Polynesia includes New Zealand, the Cook Islands, French Polynesia, Tonga, American Samoa and Western Samoa. New Zealand was a former British colony and is now a modern, industrialized nation. This distinguishes it from other Polynesian nations.

TOKELAU

Capital:	each atoll has its own administrative centre
Area:	10 km²
Population:	1,690 and 2,802 live in New Zealand
Currency:	New Zealand dollar
GNP per person ($):	n/a
Principal languages:	Tokelauan, English.

FRENCH POLYNESIA

Capital:	Papeete, on Tahiti
Area:	3,521 km²
Population:	205,800
Currency:	Polynesian French franc
GNP per person ($):	7000
Principal languages:	French, Polynesian principal languages.

TOKELAU ISLANDS

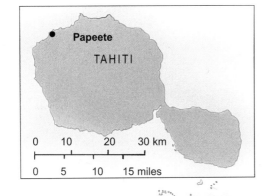

COOK ISLANDS

TAHITI FRENCH POLYNESIA

RARATONGA

PITCAIRN ISLAND GROUP

Capital:	Adamstown
Area:	35 km²
Population:	55
Currency:	New Zealand dollar, Pitcairn dollar
GNP per person ($):	n/a
Principal languages:	English, Pitcairnese.

PITCAIRN ISLANDS

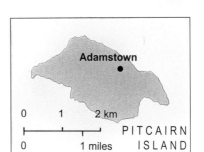

COOK ISLANDS

Capital:	Avarua, on Rarotonga
Area:	227 km²
Population:	17,000m and 26,925 Cook Islanders live in New Zealand
Currency:	New Zealand dollar and Cook Islands dollar
GNP per person ($):	n/a
Principal languages:	Cook Islands Maori, English.

EASTER ISLAND

Capital:	Hanga Roa
Area:	163 km²
Population:	2,089
Currency:	Chilean peso
GNP per person ($):	n/a
Principal languages:	Spanish.

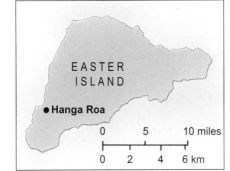

INTRODUCTION

One third of the earth's surface is covered by the Pacific Ocean, the world's largest and deepest body of water. It stretches from the western coast of North and South America eastwards to Asia and Australia. There are between 20–30,000 Pacific islands. Most are just small piles of rock or sand that jut up above the sea. Oceania is the name given to the islands located in the southern and central Pacific Ocean, most of which are uninhabited.

From the 'red centre' of the Australian outback, to the tropical coral islands of Oceania, the different environments of the region have shaped its human development.

Below A satellite photo showing Australia and Oceania.

OCEANIA

The island countries of Oceania have a combined land area of less than 1.3 million km² and a population of 12 million. The Oceanic islands fall into three broad groups based on their geographical position and the culture of their indigenous inhabitants. These groups are Melanesia, Micronesia and Polynesia.

The economy of the countries of Oceania is agricultural, although there is some mining, and tourism is a growing industry. New Zealand is an exception, and has a modern, industrialized economy. In many ways, New Zealand has more in common with Australia than with its neighbours in Oceania.

THE FORMATION OF AUSTRALIA

About 150 million years ago, the southern super-continent of Gondwanaland began to break into sections. One of these was Australia. Between 55–10 million years ago, Australia drifted north from the South Pole across the surface of the earth to its present position.

New Guinea was once part of the Australian landmass. Eight thousand years ago, as ocean levels rose throughout the world, the bridge of land that joined New Guinea to Australia was covered by water. This is now known as Torres Strait, and is the home of the Torres Strait Islanders.

The Great Barrier Reef, off the north-eastern coast of Australia, runs for more than 2,000 km. It is the longest coral reef in the world, and a popular tourist destination.

THE PACIFIC RIM

Not all the islands that lie in the Pacific Ocean are part of Oceania. The island nations of Indonesia, the Philippines and Japan are in the continent of Asia. In the eastern Pacific, the islands near North and South America are considered to be part of those continents; for example, the island of Hawaii is the fiftieth state of the USA. All the nations that border Oceania are in the Pacific Rim.

Each day, the earth turns through 360° (one complete revolution) in 24 hours. So each hour it turns through 15°. The surface of the earth is divided up into twenty-four time zones, each of 15° longitude or 1 hour of time. The times shown for each zone are the standard times kept on land and sea when it is 12 noon on the Greenwich meantime line.

The international date line cuts through the middle of Oceania. The international date line is the line approximately following the 180° meridian from Greenwich, on the east side of which the date is 1 day earlier than on the west.

Greenwich Mean Time (GMT)

5 Hours ahead of GMT

5 Hours behind GMT

Half hour zones

THE GEOGRAPHY OF AUSTRALIA AND OCEANIA

AUSTRALIA: 'THE DRY CONTINENT'

Two thirds of Australia is arid or semi-arid, so it is not surprising that it is known as 'the dry continent'. Rainfall, or the lack of it, has shaped the pattern of human settlement. Aboriginal populations were greater in regions of higher rainfall and where there were supplies of fresh water. The Aborigines managed their environment through techniques such as fire-stick farming, where new growth was encouraged by burning sections of the land. European settlement and agriculture in Australia is also concentrated around the fertile coastal regions and river valleys.

The arid west

The western half of Australia consists of a large plateau that is geologically very old. Some rocks are over 3,000 million years old. These western regions are the most arid in the continent, and there is little surface water. Here are Australia's vast deserts: the Great Sandy Desert, the Great Victoria Desert and the Nullabor Plain.

The central lowlands

Much of central Australia is very flat, but there are some mountain ranges and high rocky formations. The central lowlands are less arid than the west, with sparse vegetation and grasslands. They stretch from the Gulf of Carpentaria in the north, to the plains of the Murray-Darling river system, which drains much of the southern part of the central lowlands. Most of Australia's irrigated agricultural land is in the Murray Valley. Large lakes form from rivers in the interior, which dry up in the summer into salt plains or mud flats.

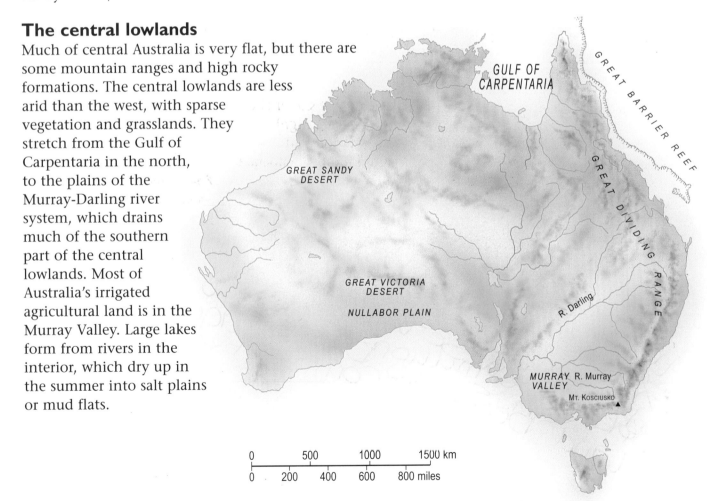

GULF OF CARPENTARIA

GREAT BARRIER REEF

GREAT DIVIDING RANGE

GREAT SANDY DESERT

GREAT VICTORIA DESERT

NULLABOR PLAIN

R. Darling

MURRAY VALLEY · R. Murray

MT. KOSCIUSKO ▲

| 0 | 500 | 1000 | 1500 km |
| 0 | 200 | 400 | 600 | 800 miles |

The eastern highlands

The eastern highlands make up about 15 per cent of Australia. They rise gently from central Australia and extend towards the coast in a series of plateaus. These form the Great Dividing Range of mountains, which runs from north to south along the eastern side of Australia. The highest point is at Mount Kosciusko (2,230 m). Snow falls in the mountainous areas in winter, but there are no permanent snowfields. In contrast to the rest of Australia, the soils of the eastern highlands are full of nutrients. The rainfall is higher, and vegetation and wildlife are extremely diverse. There are tropical rain forests, temperate forests of eucalypts, and rich agricultural and grazing lands. Most Australians live in the eastern highlands.

Above One of Australia's most striking physical features is the extraordinary rock of Uluru (Ayers Rock) which rises 335 m above the Central Desert.

Below The Tasmanian Bennett's wallaby (pictured here with its joey, as young wallabies are called) is a marsupial.

PLANT AND ANIMAL LIFE

Australian plant and animal life is varied and unique, and has adapted to the different environmental conditions. There are thousands of species of birds, such as the flightless emu and colourful parrots and cockatoos. Monotremes, such as echidnas and platypuses, produce their young by laying eggs. Kangaroos, koalas, possums and wombats are marsupials – mammals that carry their young in a pouch.

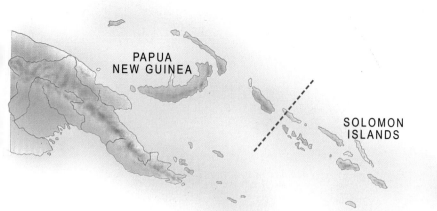

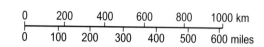

OCEANIA: TROPICAL ISLANDS

The islands of Oceania have a variety of landforms, soils, and plant and animal life. The ecosystems on each island show that the way that plants and animals both depend on, and are needed by, the environment is a very complicated process. Most islands are relatively small, and this means that any changes in the environment brought about by human activity, or nature, will effect the ecosystem. Human society in Oceania has adapted to environments as different as the dense rain forests of Papua New Guinea and the palm-fringed lagoons of tiny islands.

CONTINENTAL ISLANDS

The islands of Papua New Guinea, the Solomon Islands, Fiji and New Zealand were once part of the ancient continental platforms of Australia and Asia. They are the largest islands in Oceania and have the highest mountains. There is a good supply of fresh water and developed river systems. The soils are fertile and rich in minerals, and can support many types of vegetation and animal life. The resources on continental islands have enabled humans to develop farming and industries, such as mining and forestry.

HIGH OCEANIC ISLANDS

In Micronesia and Polynesia, many islands are 'high oceanic islands'. Their scenery is often rugged and spectacular, with steep cliffs and high waterfalls, and there are thick forests and grasslands. The soil is fertile, but usually lacking in minerals, so plant and animal life is less varied than on continental islands. Human settlement is usually restricted to the lower slopes and coastal plains.

Above *The high oceanic islands are the tops of ancient volcanoes that rise above sea-level from the ocean floor. On some islands, volcanoes are still active.*

THE IMPORTANCE OF CORAL

Many islands are formed from the build-up of coral. Over millions of years, coral reefs, made from the skeletons of millions of tiny sea animals, became attached to a core of land or rock that rose above the surface of the ocean. When the island core was flooded, as the level of the world's oceans rose, the coral reef continued to grow outwards.

Newer reefs were formed further from shore, and were separated from the island by a lagoon. A coral atoll is formed when the coral reef eventually makes a circle around the lagoon. In time, the reef will support a number of small islets of reef debris that may be up to 9 m above sea level. These islets are known locally as *motus*.

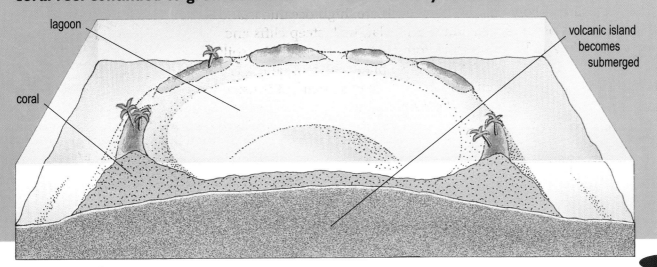

lagoon

coral

volcanic island
becomes
submerged

THE WEATHER
Australia

Half of Australia has less than 300 mm annual rainfall. In some areas, there may be no rain for years. The lowest rainfall is recorded at Lake Eyre. Every 30 years or so, rain turns its dry saltpans into a lake brimming with water. Yet Australia's climate can also be alpine or tropical. The wettest place is Tully, on the north-east coast, where the average annual rainfall is more than 4,000 mm. In the south-east, the climate is temperate and rainfall patterns are less extreme. Temperatures differ according to season and environment. Average annual temperatures range from 28 °C to 4 °C. It can get as hot as 50 °C in some places! July is the coldest month, and January and February are the hottest.

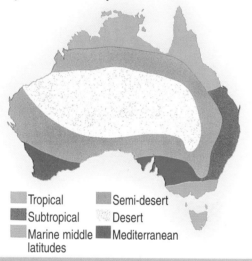

Tropical Semi-desert
Subtropical Desert
Marine middle Mediterranean
latitudes

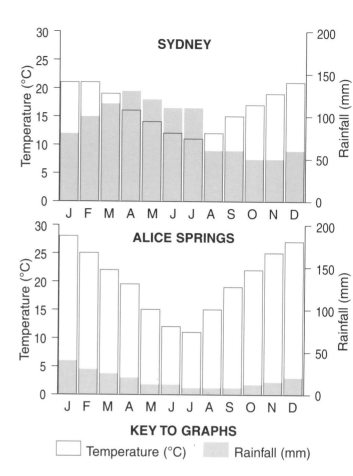

SYDNEY

ALICE SPRINGS

KEY TO GRAPHS
☐ Temperature (°C)   ▨ Rainfall (mm)

Above *Temperature and rainfall graphs for Sydney, with a pleasant, temperate climate, and Alice Springs, which is uncomfortably hot and dry.*

Left *Australian climate/vegetation zones.*

NATURAL HAZARDS

Floods, droughts and bushfires happen regularly in Australia. Since the 1860s, there have been nine major droughts. The most recent, in 1992–1995, affected most of the continent. Crops failed, and millions of sheep and cattle starved to death, or were so weak that farmers had to shoot them. When heavy rains finally broke the drought, flooding occurred in some areas.

    Almost all vegetation types in Australia are prone to fire. In fact, fire is a natural part of the Australian environment and some plant seeds will only germinate after fire. But seasonal bushfires cause great damage to property and crops. The authorities in Australia are working to develop new fire-fighting techniques to cope with future fire disasters.

Below *There have been several major bushfires in recent decades. In January 1994, fires reached the suburbs of Sydney and these houses at West Como were burnt out.*

Oceania

The climate of Oceania is influenced by the islands' position in the Pacific Ocean. Most islands are tropical, with average temperatures between 20 °C–27 °C and high humidity. There are usually distinct wet and dry seasons that last for several months. The highest mountains in New Guinea and New Zealand are covered in snow throughout the year.

The seasonal circular winds of tropical cyclones cause much of the rainfall in the Pacific region. Occasionally, the winds become very strong. When they exceed 119 km per hour, they are called typhoons or hurricanes. At the centre, or 'eye' of the hurricane, the speed of the wind may be 240 km per hour. Hurricanes cause extensive damage at sea, where they produce enormous waves that can submerge ships and completely cover low islands. On land, hurricanes destroy crops and buildings.

Above Some islands have an average of over 3,800 mm of rain a year. Here on Rarotonga, in the Cook Islands, the islanders are working on flood control measures.

Below The different regions in which precipitation is enhanced (dashed lines) and diminished (solid lines) by the Southern Oscillation. The months in which the regions are affected generally coincide with the local rainy season.

THE SOUTHERN OSCILLATION

The weather in Australia and Oceania is shaped by the see-sawing, or up and down motion, of atmospheric pressure between northern Australia and the central Pacific Ocean. This is known as oscillation. Meteorologists have set up the Southern Oscillation Index to measure the 'highs' and 'lows' of this atmospheric pressure. Many of the extremes of climate in the region are caused by these movements in the atmosphere.

The Index measures the difference in pressure between Darwin, in northern Australia, and Tahiti. If the pressure is very high in Darwin and very low in Tahiti, it is likely there will be droughts in northern and eastern Australia. But if the pressure is very low in Darwin and very high in Tahiti, rainfall levels in Australia will be well above average.

THE HISTORY OF AUSTRALIA AND OCEANIA

The prehistory (history before writing) of humans in Australia dates back at least 50,000 years. The first people came from south-east Asia. They gradually spread throughout the continent and into New Guinea, which was joined to Australia until 8,000 years ago. Archaeologists believe that all of Australia was occupied about 25,000 years ago.

About 4,000 years ago, people from south-east Asia began to arrive by boat in parts of Melanesia. From Melanesia, long sea voyages extended into Polynesia and Micronesia. Over time, settlement of the islands occurred. Distinctive cultures evolved throughout the region. These were shaped both by the physical environment of each island and how isolated they were from neighbouring cultures.

People in Oceania developed sophisticated technology for managing their environments. Canoes were used for fishing and provided access to other islands. Tools were made of bone, stone and shell. Fruit trees and tuber plants were grown, and pigs, dogs and chickens were raised. Religious and artistic life was rich and varied.

EASTER ISLAND

The Rapu Nui people call their home on Easter Island 'the navel of the world'. Easter Island was inhabited 2,000 years ago by immigrants from Polynesia, and a thriving civilization developed. From AD 400–1600, stone platforms and 600 gigantic stone statues, known as Moais, were carved from volcanic rock using sophisticated technology and artistic skill.

The largest Moais is 12 m tall, but an unfinished one is almost double that height. Today, it would take 15 months for two teams of masons, working in shifts, to carve a medium-sized statue. Over one hundred workers would be needed to move the statue from the quarry and erect it elsewhere on the island. No-one knows why the faces of the Moais were always turned away from the sea, or why the people of Easter Island stopped carving them.

EUROPEAN INVASION

By the late fifteenth century, Europeans were exploring the globe looking for 'New Worlds'. In 1513, the Spanish explorer Vasco Nunez de Balboa was the first European to sight the Pacific Ocean. Ferdinand Magellan sailed around South America and across the Pacific in 1520. Over the next two centuries, Spanish, Dutch, and British voyages located several island groups, including New Zealand. By the late eighteenth century, the three voyages of James Cook filled in most of the gaps in the European map of Oceania.

European and American missionaries, whalers and traders invaded the Oceanic islands during the nineteenth century. The traders were after goods such as coconut oil, sandalwood and pearl shell. Trading communities and port towns sprang up. Europeans began to establish plantations to grow cotton and sugar, and to use the land for grazing and agriculture. By the end of the nineteenth century, the islands were under the control of the colonial powers of Britain, France, Germany and the USA.

The Europeans brought new diseases to the societies of Oceania, and thousands of indigenous peoples died as a result. Europeans also brought guns. War broke out in some islands, including New Zealand, when indigenous peoples resisted Europeans who were taking their land. European colonization of Oceania stripped indigenous societies of their land and its resources, and their political power.

EUROPEAN EXPANSION INTO AUSTRALIA

■ Areas occupied by 1850

■ Areas occupied by 1890

ABORIGINES

Prior to the British invasion in 1788, there were between 750,000–3 million Aborigines in Australia. They lived in about 650 groups, and each group had its own political and social organization, language and territory. There was no single Aboriginal way of life, because the different environments influenced daily life. Trade and seasonal ceremonies brought groups together. Each group managed its land and resources without damaging the environment.

British invasion was disastrous for Australia's indigenous populations. Although they fought back, Aborigines were driven from their lands to missions and reserves. European massacres and diseases caused thousands of deaths. By 1900, Aboriginal populations had decreased to 50,000.

THE SETTLEMENT OF AUSTRALIA

In 1606, a Dutch explorer, named Willem Jansz, was the first European to land in Australia. The Dutch soon mapped most of the coastline of the land they called 'New Holland'. The British navigator James Cook landed at Botany Bay in 1770, and took possession of the land for Britain.

In 1788, the British sent convicts to establish a colony at Botany Bay, near Sydney. Free immigrants followed, hungry for land. By the 1830s, wool was an important export. The discovery of gold in the 1850s attracted further immigrants, and the white population tripled in a decade.

Australia was settled as six British colonies: New South Wales, Victoria, Tasmania, South Australia, Western Australia and Queensland. In 1901, the colonies became a national government.

GOVERNMENT

Modern forms of government in Australia and Oceania have evolved from the region's colonial history. Nations that formerly were British colonies, for example, have adopted systems of government based on the British parliamentary system. This means that the population democratically elects representatives to the parliament. Yet, traditional kinship ties in Pacific societies have also contributed to the style of modern politics in Oceania.

In 1901, the six British colonies in Australia adopted a federal constitution and became one nation. The federal parliament consists of an upper house (the Senate) and a lower house (the House of Representatives). The head of state is the governor-general, who represents the British monarch. But the real power is held by the cabinet and prime minister, who represent the political party with the majority in the House of Representatives. There are two further levels of government: elected parliaments in each state, and a system of local government. It is compulsory for Australians over 18 years to vote.

TWO WORLD WARS

During the twentieth century, Australia has maintained its economic and cultural links with Britain, and fought with the Allies in two world wars. In December 1941, war came to the Oceanic region after the Japanese bombed Pearl Harbour, in Hawaii. By 1942, Japanese troops had captured much of New Guinea and the Solomons. Australian, American and other Allied troops, helped by indigenous peoples, drove the Japanese from the islands. The Japanese surrendered in September 1945. The war had a considerable cultural impact on Oceania and exposed remote island societies to Europeans.

Left *Left-over tanks and guns on Saipan, in the Mariana Islands, are reminders of the Second World War in the Pacific.*

In New Zealand today, the British monarch (represented by a governor-general) is the head of state, but like Australia, the elected parliament, its cabinet and prime minister make the governmental decisions. The New Zealand parliament consists of the House of Representatives. A few parliamentary seats are reserved for Maori candidates and voters. Maori are the indigenous Polynesian peoples of New Zealand, who make up approximately 13 % of the total population.

In the 1960s, most of the nations of Oceania were demanding independence from the five foreign nations – Britain, France, the USA, New Zealand and Australia – who administered them. By the 1990s, all nations in Oceania had gained some form of political independence. Fully independent nations such as Kiribati, Nauru, Papua New Guinea, Western Samoa, the Solomon Islands, Tuvalu and Vanuatu now have democratically elected parliaments, led by a prime minister.

The French Overseas Territories of French Polynesia, New Caledonia and Wallis and Futuna have some self-government, and elect representatives to the French parliament. In French Polynesia and New Caledonia there are popular movements demanding full independence from France.

According to some 'free association' agreements, island states are responsible for their own government, but leave decisions about international affairs to larger nations. New Zealand is responsible for external affairs in the Cook Islands and Niue. In 1986, the Marshall Islands and the Federated States of Micronesia gained the status of 'free association' with the USA. The North Mariana Islands are a commonwealth of the USA, while Guam remains US territory.

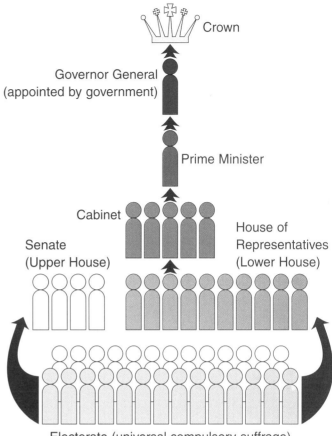

Above The Australian government structure, 1996.

Below King Taufa'ahau Toupou IV of Tonga, who came to the throne in 1965.

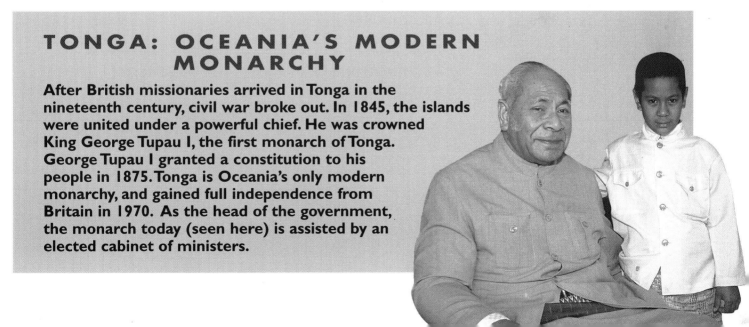

TONGA: OCEANIA'S MODERN MONARCHY

After British missionaries arrived in Tonga in the nineteenth century, civil war broke out. In 1845, the islands were united under a powerful chief. He was crowned King George Tupau I, the first monarch of Tonga. George Tupau I granted a constitution to his people in 1875. Tonga is Oceania's only modern monarchy, and gained full independence from Britain in 1970. As the head of the government, the monarch today (seen here) is assisted by an elected cabinet of ministers.

THE PEOPLES OF AUSTRALIA AND OCEANIA

POPULATION

The populations of Australia and Oceania are among the most culturally diverse of any region in the world. Before European colonization, there were more than 1,500 separate indigenous societies spread throughout the Australian continent and the islands of the Pacific. Since then, European and Asian immigration to Australia and Oceania has contributed to the region's populations.

Physical geography has determined the distribution of settlement in Australia and Oceania. In recent decades, there have been population movements from rural areas to towns and cities. Most nations in Oceania are predominantly rural, but Australia is one of the most urbanized countries in the world. Eighty-five per cent of Australians are urban-dwellers, with thirty-nine per cent of the population living in the two cities of Sydney (3.7 million) and Melbourne (3.2 million). The state capitals of Brisbane, Adelaide and Perth all have populations of more than 1 million.

AUSTRALIAN POPULATION DENSITIES

Darwin
Brisbane
Sydney
Perth
Canberra
Melbourne
Hobart

Inhabitants per km²

Over 100
50-100
25-50
12-25
3-12
1-3
Under 1

Above *Australia's population is concentrated on the south-east coast.*

AN IMMIGRANT NATION

All non-indigenous Australians are either immigrants or the descendants of immigrants who came to Australia over the past 200 years. Until 1945, about ninety-eight per cent of the Australian population was of British or Irish origin. After the Second World War, there was a labour shortage in Australia and the government established schemes to attract workers from Europe. Immigrants came from northern, eastern and southern Europe, and from Turkey and Lebanon.

By the 1970s, immigrants came from Asia, particularly from Vietnam and Laos. A policy of multiculturalism recognizes the cultural diversity of the Australian population. It is illegal to discriminate against persons because of their race, and Australia is proud of its multicultural population.

Below *This Vietnamese community is in Sydney, New South Wales. Many Vietnamese immigrants were refugees from war, who came in search of a better life. Ethnic communities with shops, places of worship, and clubs have been established in Australian cities.*

ABORIGINES AND TORRES STRAIT ISLANDERS

Australia has two indigenous peoples: Aborigines and Torres Strait Islanders. Their numbers decreased dramatically during the colonial period, but began to grow during the twentieth century. In 1991, 1.6 per cent of the total Australian population, or 265,459 people, were of indigenous origin. Only about 24,000 of these were Torres Strait Islanders, most of whom live in Queensland. Aboriginal populations are concentrated in the northern and central regions of Australia, and in northern New South Wales. In the Northern Territory, more than one-in-five people are of Aboriginal origin.

In the twentieth century, Aborigines have been demanding the return of their lands and human rights. This protest march took place in Sydney on Australia Day, 1988.

FROM *TERRA NULLIUS* TO NATIVE TITLE

When the British settled in Australia, they claimed it was *terra nullius* (unoccupied). In 1967, Aborigines were granted citizenship and could vote for the first time. It was not until a High Court judgement in 1992 that Australians legally recognized that Aborigines had native title (rights of ownership) of their traditional lands. The Australian government is working towards reconciliation between Aborigines and non-Aboriginal society. In 1993, the Native Title Act was passed. It will return land to some Aboriginal groups and compensate others. The Native Title Act will involve negotiations between Aboriginal groups, farmers and mining companies over land.

THE PEOPLES OF OCEANIA

Approximately 12 million people live in Oceania, but only New Zealand and Papua New Guinea have populations above 1 million. The population of most of the Oceanic islands is in the thousands, and only fifty-five people live on Pitcairn Island. Most Oceanic peoples still live in farming and fishing villages. However, more people are moving to towns, cities and other islands – especially New Zealand – in search of employment. This trend has placed a strain on housing and other facilities in urban centres.

In the colonial period, most indigenous populations decreased due to European diseases and warfare. More recently, better healthcare and education have resulted in relatively high population growth. In Papua New Guinea, annual population growth is 2.7 per cent.

The natural resources on some smaller islands are not sufficient to support rapid population increases. Over-population has posed a problem since the 1970s. In Kiribati, for example, over-population means it is likely that about 5,000 people will be forced to settle elsewhere during the 1990s. Population has been kept to a manageable size in the Cook Islands and Niue through immigration to New Zealand. In fact, more Cook Islanders and Niueans live in New Zealand than on their home islands.

For their traditional 'sing sing', the Huli Wigmen of Papua New Guinea wear colourful feathers and paint their faces.

THE MAORI

Aotearoa is the Maori name for New Zealand. Maori are Polynesian people whose ancestors came to New Zealand more than 1,000 years ago. At the time of European contact in 1769, there were about 200,000 Maori. The impact of colonization reduced their numbers to 42,000 by 1896, but by the middle of the twentieth century, Maori populations began to increase significantly.

Today, 13 per cent of New Zealand's population of 3.5 million are Maori. The majority are urban dwellers. A further 5 per cent of the population are Polynesians from the Cook Islands, Niue and Western Samoa. The city of Auckland has the highest Polynesian population in the world.

Maori is now an official language of New Zealand and is used in schools, universities and the media. There is a greater awareness of Maori culture among white New Zealanders, and Maori have been politically active in demanding greater access to services and rights to land.

These Maori women are exchanging a traditional greeting known as hongi.

The indigenous peoples of Oceania form three ethnic and cultural groups known as Melanesians, Micronesians and Polynesians. They generally live in the three geographical areas of the same names. However, there is great diversity in the customs, physical appearance and language within each of these groups. This is demonstrated by the number of languages in Oceania. Approximately 1,200 of the world's 3,000 languages are spoken here. There are more than 740 separate languages in Papua New Guinea alone, about thirteen major languages in Micronesia and twenty in Polynesia.

During the last two centuries, immigrants have come to Oceania from Europe, the USA and Asia. There are tiny 'foreign' populations of immigrants on most islands. In New Caledonia, 37 per cent of the population is of French origin. In New Zealand, 78 per cent of the population is of European, mainly British, descent. In some societies, there has been considerable intermarriage between indigenous peoples and European and Asian immigrants.

RELIGION

Ancient Aboriginal societies held religious beliefs about the creation of the land, its animals and plants, during a time called the 'Dreamtime'. Each Aboriginal group had Dreamtime histories and ceremonies dealing with the creation of their own territory. Every territory had places of religious significance, known as sacred sites. Spiritual beliefs laid the foundation for the political and social organization of Aboriginal life.

Today, the religious relationship between people and their land remains important to Aborigines and some groups still practise traditional beliefs. Others have become Christians.

Traditional religions among the societies of Oceania vary considerably, but religion is still an important force in everyday life. In Polynesia and Micronesia, In Polynesia and Micronesia, there are complex religious beliefs and mythologies. These are associated with traditional family structures and authority and powers of hereditary chiefs.

In the diverse societies of Melanesia, the worship of ancestor spirits is widespread. Spirits are a force in daily life, and religion is linked closely to magic. Elaborate religious ceremonies are held to mark trading and kinship relationships.

CHRISTIANITY

The introduction of Christianity has eroded many traditional religious beliefs. By the nineteenth century, Protestants and Roman Catholic missionaries had established bases throughout Oceania. Their activities were very successful and the nations of Oceania are now among the most Christian in the world.

In converting the indigenous people to Christianity, the missionaries brought great social and political change. They introduced European education, health services and agricultural practices. Although some missionaries were sympathetic to indigenous peoples, overall they were responsible for much destruction of the Melanesian, Polynesian and Micronesian cultures.

Above *Missionaries continue to work in some of the remote regions of Papua New Guinea. This is the Kegsugl Catholic Mission in the Chimbu area, with Mount Wilhelm in the background.*

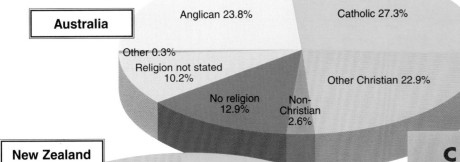

Australia

Anglican 23.8%
Catholic 27.3%
Other 0.3%
Religion not stated 10.2%
Other Christian 22.9%
No religion 12.9%
Non-Christian 2.6%

New Zealand

Anglican 24.7%
Catholic 15.0%
Religion not stated 7.6%
Other Christian 30.5%
No religion 20.1%
Non-Christian 2.1%

Above *In the 1991 census, 74 per cent of Australians and 70 per cent of New Zealanders listed their religion as Christian. There are also small numbers of Muslims, Hindus, Buddhists and Jews.*

CARGO CULTS

One effect of European colonization on traditional religions in Oceania can be seen in the development of cargo cults in Melanesia. These religious movements believe that ancestor spirits will deliver large quantities of modern, Westernized goods by plane or ship to their believers. Cargo cults often have political purposes that are directed against European influences.

HUMAN DEVELOPMENT IN AUSTRALIA AND OCEANIA

Australia's mostly urban population live in Westernized housing, usually with a garden. There has been an increasing trend towards higher density housing in cities. The majority of people own their own homes, although this proportion is declining.

The environment has shaped the architecture of some Australian housing. In tropical areas, houses are elevated on stilts to allow greater air circulation. In the opal-mining town of Coober Pedy, in the interior, it is so hot that houses are built underground.

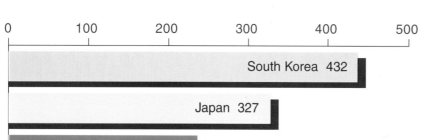

| 0 | 100 | 200 | 300 | 400 | 500 |

South Korea 432

Japan 327

Britain 234

China 119

USA 27

New Zealand 13

Australia 2

Above *Australia has one of the lowest population densities in the world. This chart shows the number of people per km^2 in Australia compared with the rest of the world.*

Source: Philips Geographical Digest 1996-97

Right *About 40 per cent of Australia's population live in Sydney and Melbourne, and one feature of these cities is their sprawling suburbs. The business districts of Melbourne and Sydney, on the other hand, are crammed with towering office blocks. This is the Chifley Tower in Sydney.*

In rural villages throughout the islands, houses are still built in traditional styles. They usually have a wooden frame, with thatched walls and roof. This house in Yap, Micronesia, is built on short stilts.

There are few cities and towns of any significant size in Oceania. The biggest cities are in New Zealand: Auckland has a population of 880,000 people. The largest city outside New Zealand is Port Morseby in Papua New Guinea (152,000 people). Apia in Western Samoa, Suva in Fiji, and Papeete in French Polynesia are major regional towns.

All towns in Oceania are growing rapidly, as people come in search of employment. The population of Port Moresby is increasing at a rate of 6 per cent each year. Shanty towns have sprung up on the outskirts of cities. Poor sanitation, overcrowding, crime and unemployment have all contributed to an increase in urban poverty. A number of Oceanic governments have responded to these social problems by building inexpensive housing.

Housing in the towns and cities of Oceania resembles those in Western countries. In New Zealand, the average urban home is of one storey with enough land for a garden, but as the population of New Zealand's cities continues to grow, more multi-storied apartment blocks are being built.

OK TEDI, PAPUA NEW GUINEA

Mining in Papua New Guinea has had financial benefits for the country, but has also caused disruption of village life and damage to the environment. The Australian-based company, BHP, controls the Ok Tedi copper mine, in the remote jungle region of the Star Mountains, in the Western Province.

The mine now provides 20 per cent of Papua New Guinea's export earnings. But protestors against the mine claim that 'Ok Tedi is not OK'. In 1984, a dam, which was to hold waste products from the mine, collapsed in a landslide. Since then, the mining operations have released poisonous or dangerous substances into the Ok Tedi river, where they are carried downstream into the Fly River. The build-up of silt and waste products has led to frequent flooding and damage to agricultural land. Pollution has killed fish, and environmentalists claim the Ok Tedi river is now biologically dead.

EDUCATION

Literacy levels are extremely high in Australia and New Zealand, and compulsory education systems have been in operation since the late nineteenth century. Education is free in government schools, and some financial assistance is provided for tertiary students. In Australia, almost 80 per cent of students graduate from secondary school, and more than half of these enter universities and vocational colleges.

Above *Both Australia and New Zealand have introduced educational programmes to serve the needs of their populations. School of the Air allows children in remote areas to study through correspondence and speak to their teachers and classmates on the radio.*

Australia has thirty-six universities. Some of these are considered among the best in the world. There has been a growing trend for students to come from overseas, mainly from Southeast Asia, to take advantage of the educational system. New Zealand has seven universities.

Missionaries introduced Western education to some of the islands of Oceania during the nineteenth century. This replaced traditional forms of education, where young people learnt artistic and practical skills from their elders. Today, all nations in Oceania provide compulsory and free education until the ages of 14 or 16 years. Few students can afford to continue their education further. Those who can must often travel to another island, or to Australia or New Zealand, since only Guam, Fiji, Papua New Guinea and Western Samoa have universities or vocational colleges. The University of the South Pacific, which is based in Fiji, also teaches via a satellite-network throughout the region.

Below *These Aboriginal school children are in Australia's Northern Territory. Some Aboriginal children are taught in their own language as well as English. In New Zealand, since the 1970s, Maori language and culture have been taught in schools with Maori students.*

Limited educational opportunities in Oceania created a professional class. European-style education systems have also meant that English or French are used before indigenous languages.

AN DEPARTMENT OF EDUCATION
ERN TERRITORY DIVISION
DIA MOBILE
No1

HEALTHCARE

In both Australia and New Zealand, there is a full range of private and public healthcare. A significant part of the countries' money is devoted to healthcare, medical training and research. Australia's medical research is internationally acclaimed.

While most Australians enjoy the benefits of their health system, few Aboriginal communities have had access to these facilities. The life expectancy of Aborigines is lower than that of the non-Aboriginal population. A National Aboriginal Health Strategy has been introduced by the government to improve the health of the Aboriginal population. New Zealand is also focusing on improved medical care for the Maori people.

The availability of health services on Oceanic islands depends upon the size and wealth of individual countries. Basic health services are free. Each nation has at least one public hospital. Fiji has a particularly well-developed medical system, and provides a wide range of services and training. Papua New Guinea spends a large amount of money educating villagers about health issues, which is reducing the numbers of deaths among mothers and infants.

Modern lifestyles have created some of the major health problems in Oceania. In traditional societies, people depended on the sea and local plants for their food. Such diets were balanced and healthy, and are still maintained in the more remote rural areas. However, the growing population, together with more land being used for cash crops for export rather than to farm food for local people, has meant that canned food has been needed on some islands. A reliance on low-protein, processed food has resulted in malnutrition, diabetes and heart disease among the population.

Above *People enjoying the hot sunshine on Bondi Beach, Australia. The sun presents a serious health risk in Australia, where there is the highest rate of skin cancer in the world. Successful health campaigns have persuaded Australians to change their attitudes to the sun and its effects, and to use protective creams.*

Right *In remote parts of the Australian outback, people rely on the Flying Doctor Service for medical care.*

RESOURCES

FARMING AND FISHING IN AUSTRALIA

The Australian economy developed during the nineteenth century as a producer of wool and meat, but today only 5 per cent of the working population are employed in farming. Most Australians now work in manufacturing and in service industries.

The arid nature of much of the Australian continent means that only 60 per cent of the land area is used for farming. Crops are grown on just 4 per cent of this and the rest is grazing land for sheep and cattle. Agriculture and grazing provide 23 per cent of all exports.

Below The map shows the main forms of agriculture practised in different parts of Australia.

Above Australia remains the world's leading producer of wool, and more than 850,000 tonnes are collected each year from the 138 million sheep.

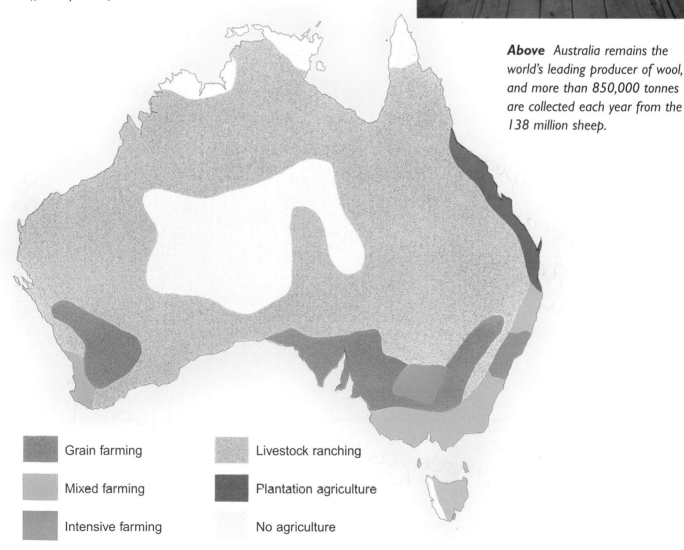

Grain farming

Mixed farming

Intensive farming

Livestock ranching

Plantation agriculture

No agriculture

Most Australian agriculture is carried out on the fertile soils of the eastern highlands. The most important crop is wheat, and the bulk of this is exported. Other cereal crops are barley and rice. A great variety of fruit and vegetables is grown. Cotton and sugar are farmed in the tropical regions. Asia is a growing market for agricultural produce.

Australia's fishing zone covers 9 million km^2 (the third-largest fishing zone in the world), but Australia's fishing industry is relatively small. Despite a huge number of marine species, only a hundred are fished commercially. The most important fishing exports are prawns, lobsters, abalone, tuna, oysters and pearls. These are mainly sold to Japan. There has been a recent growth in aquaculture (marine farming) of oysters, freshwater trout and crocodiles.

OVERSEAS MARKETS

Australia's farming production is influenced by overseas markets. A major factor in the agricultural development of Australia is the General Agreement on Tariffs and Trade (GATT), signed in 1993. In this, agricultural producers throughout the world agreed to reduce tariffs, or taxes, on imports. This makes Australian agricultural exports more competitive: it is estimated they will increase by about A$5 billion each year.

Although livestock numbers declined in the early 1990s, today there are 24 million cattle in Australia, which is a major exporter of beef.

OCEANIA

The small size of most of the islands in Oceania means that there is little potential to develop agriculture on a large scale. Under colonial rule, much of the agricultural land was owned by Europeans. Today, agricultural production is usually on small, family-owned farms and livestock is usually raised for local consumption.

Intensive farming is possible on the fertile soils of the continental islands, but on the coral islands, agriculture is at the level of subsistence. This means that only enough food is grown to feed the local population, and few people receive cash in exchange for crops. On some islands, the agricultural production is so low, and populations have grown so rapidly, that food has to be imported. The Federated States of Micronesia and Kiribati both depend on foreign aid and food imports to feed their populations.

Above On Rarotonga in the Cook Islands, land has been cleared for growing pawpaw trees.

Below Agriculture in Oceania: there is little variation in farming outside of New Zealand. Other, smaller islands produce mainly cash crops, such as fruit, if their farming goes beyond people growing food for themselves.

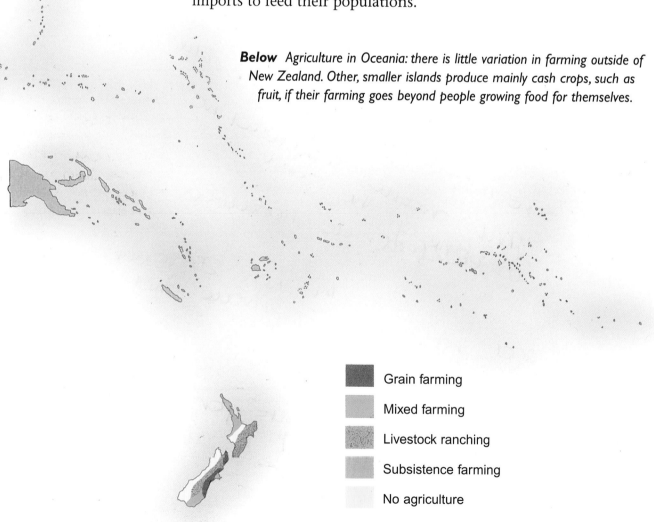

- Grain farming
- Mixed farming
- Livestock ranching
- Subsistence farming
- No agriculture

The most important agricultural export in Oceania is copra, the dried meat of the coconut palm. Factories crush copra to produce coconut oil, which is exported around the world for use in the manufacture of products such as margarine and soap. The economies of Tonga, Western Samoa, the Cook Islands, Vanuatu and the Marshall Islands rely heavily on the export of copra and coconut oil.

Other agricultural exports include pineapples, bananas, cocoa, coffee, vanilla beans, ginger, palm oil and spices. Sugar is a major export industry in Fiji. Small quantities of timber and wood products are also exported from some nations.

Commercial fishing techniques are expensive and need modern ships. In the Pacific deep-sea fishing for tuna is carried out by foreign fleets. Canning factories have opened in American Samoa, Fiji and the Solomon Islands.

Above This tuna-canning factory at Levuka, Ovalau Island in Fiji, provides local employment and contributes to the nation's economy.

NEW ZEALAND: 'THE WORLD'S BIGGEST FARM'

Although New Zealand is sometimes called 'the world's biggest farm', much of the land is not naturally arable. The success of New Zealand's agriculture has depended upon management of the grasslands and the use of fertilizers and machinery. Agricultural products account for almost 50 per cent of New Zealand's exports. Cereal crops are grown for local consumption. Fruit and vegetables are exported, including tropical varieties like avocados and tamarillos.

About 53 per cent of the land is used for crops and pastureland. Sheep and cattle are raised for meat, wool, hides and dairy produce. There are about 20 times as many sheep as people in New Zealand! In 1992, there were 53 million sheep, 4.6 million beef cattle and 3.5 million dairy cattle. In recent years, deer and goats have also been farmed.

Below New Zealand is the world's largest producer of kiwifruit. This fruit has a furry, brown skin and a bright green centre, and takes its name from the kiwi, a flightless native bird that has become New Zealand's national symbol.

MINERAL RESOURCES AND INDUSTRY IN AUSTRALIA

Australia's immense mineral resources have always been exploited. The Aborigines mined and traded in ochre. The discovery of gold in the nineteenth century attracted thousands of European immigrants. During the twentieth century, Australia's mineral resources have been further explored, and towns have been established around mines. Oil and natural gas deposits have also been found. Minerals now account for 40 per cent of all Australian exports, making A$29 billion a year.

After the Second World War, industry expanded in Australia, but in the last twenty years, the manufacturing sector has decreased. Today, only about 15 per cent of the working population are involved in manufacturing. Traditional industries such as textiles have declined, while the production of metals has expanded. Australia imports many goods, including machinery, vehicles, petroleum products and computer technology. In 1993, the value of imports to Australia was A$59.6 billion.

The majority of the Australian population is now employed in service industries. These include retail, community services, finance, property and business agencies, and government administration.

This iron ore mine is at Roolan Island in Western Australia. In addition to iron ore, coal, gold, copper, lead, zinc, tin, uranium and diamonds are also mined in the region.

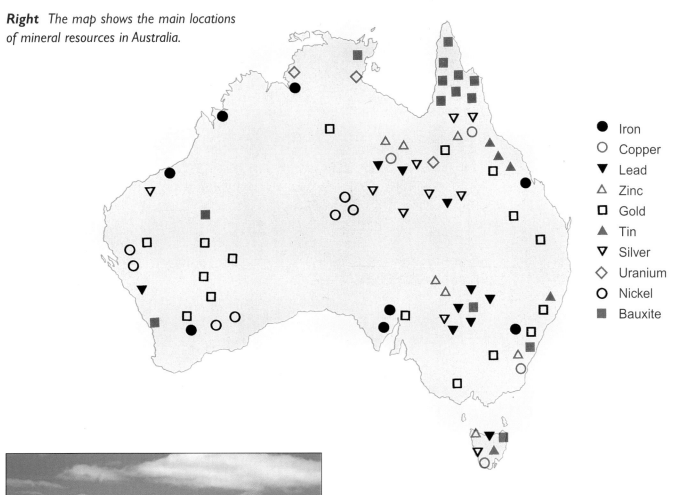

Right The map shows the main locations of mineral resources in Australia.

● Iron
○ Copper
▼ Lead
△ Zinc
□ Gold
▲ Tin
▽ Silver
◇ Uranium
◯ Nickel
■ Bauxite

Left The world's longest stretch of straight railway track runs for 475 km, on the route from Perth in Western Australia, across the Nullabor Plain, to Adelaide in South Australia.

COMMUNICATIONS

One of the most important factors in the economic development of Australia and Oceania is the region's geographical isolation. There are huge distances between cities and towns in Australia. There are even greater distances between some of the islands in the Pacific, but modern technologies have brought the region closer together, and into greater contact with the rest of the world. Telephones, television, satellite communications and air transport have been particularly important.

Australia and New Zealand have well-established systems of roads, railways and air transport. There is a high proportion of vehicle ownership, and several international airports. While roads are poor on some of the small Pacific islands, this is rapidly changing. The tourist industry has emphasized the need for improved transport and communications.

MINERAL RESOURCES AND INDUSTRY IN OCEANIA

Only the larger islands in Oceania have significant deposits of minerals. New Caledonia has large deposits of nickel, chromium, cobalt, iron and magnesium. Gold and copper are mined in Papua New Guinea, Fiji and the Solomon Islands. New Zealand is alone in Oceania in having a developed industrial base. Its manufacturing industries make up 21 per cent of the national economy and employ almost 25 per cent of all workers. Industries include the production of steel and aluminium, textiles and food processing.

Lack of money, foreign investment and a skilled workforce means industry is limited throughout the rest of Oceania. There is small-scale manufacturing in some larger towns, where mills and factories produce coconut products, soap and sugar. Most nations rely very heavily on imports of foods, vehicles and other manufactured goods. The value of imports is much more than exports.

PHOSPHATE MINING IN NAURU

The economy of Nauru is based on the mining of phosphate (a chemical used in fertilizer). The export of phosphate has brought the Nauruans a high standard of living, but 80 per cent of their island (21 km²) is destroyed. The mined areas of Nauru look like a barren moonscape. There are no birds and there is no vegetation. Over 10 thousand Nauruans live on the small unmined section of the island.

On Nauru, about 2 million tonnes of phosphate are extracted each year. Although the island has become rich through mining, it has been laid bare and stripped of most foliage.

For most of the twentieth century, the phosphate industry was British owned, and Australia was responsible for the administration of Nauru. In 1968, Nauru became an independent nation, and gained control of its own resources. Australia has agreed to pay A$107 million to Nauru as compensation for the environmental damage caused by mining. This money will be used to rehabilitate the mined areas. The phosphate is expected to run out by the year 2000, so the government of Nauru is developing alternative industries, such as finance, fishing and shipping.

Right About 20 per cent of the world's nickel reserves are in New Caledonia. The nickel ore is extracted from open-cast mines and refined at a smelter before being exported.

● Iron
○ Copper
△ Zinc
□ Gold
▽ Silver
⊙ Nickel
△ Phosphate

Above The map shows the main locations of mineral resources in Oceania.

MINERAL WEALTH IN PAPUA NEW GUINEA

About 80 per cent of the population in Papua New Guinea are subsistence farmers. In the past, crops such as coffee and cocoa provided the main source of export revenue, but in recent years deposits of gold, copper, silver, oil and natural gas have been found. By the 1980s, mining accounted for at least 20 per cent of all government revenue. One of the largest copper mines in the world is at Panguma on the island of Bougainville. In 1989, the mine was closed when local people demanded a greater share of the mining revenue and independence from the Papua New Guinea government.

THE ENVIRONMENT

Here on Papua New Guinea, natural forest has been cleared for growing crops. This is just a small patch of land, but increasingly large areas are also being stripped, leading to environmental problems.

European agricultural and grazing techniques have caused serious environmental problems in Australia. Soils are eroding and their salt levels are rising. Introduced plants and animals have taken over from native species. Many native plants, birds and mammals in Australia are now extinct, or are in danger of becoming so. The Australian government is funding programmes of land care and regeneration, but the environmental effects of over 200 years of abuse may be impossible to reverse.

Oceania also has its share of environmental problems. On some islands, natural resources, such as timber, have been exploited with little concern for the future. Growing populations also place pressure on limited resources. Like Australia, the nations of Oceania must aim towards programmes of sustainable development in the future.

ATOMIC TESTING

Both Australia and Oceania have been used as sites for the testing of atomic bombs by foreign powers. In the 1950s and 1960s, British tests were held in remote parts of Australia and in Polynesia. The USA blew up Bikini and Enewetak Atolls in Micronesia. In 1963, the USA and Britain agreed to stop testing, but two years later the French began. By 1991, they had conducted 165 tests on Mururoa and Fangataufa Atolls in French Polynesia. In 1995, France's President Chirac announced further tests would be held before an international ban on nuclear testing, to be introduced in 1996.

VIOLENT PROTEST

On 5 September 1995, the French resumed testing of nuclear weapons at Mururoa Atoll in French Polynesia. Following the nuclear blast, more than 1,000 Tahitians took over the airport outside Papeete and burned down the building in protest. Violence erupted, with the French police arresting many of the protestors. One of these was Oscar Temaru, the leader of Tahiti's Tavini party, which seeks political independence from France.

Temaru believes that the protests in Papeete were a sign that 'a whole people had risen to demonstrate' against French nuclear testing in the South Pacific. Temaru, and many other Polynesians, believe that the French have ignored the wishes of the indigenous peoples of French Polynesia, and have done little to stimulate the local economy so that it is less dependent on French imports and money.

The bombs tested over Mururoa were 100 times larger than the bomb dropped on Hiroshima in 1945. Scientists are in debate about the effects on the environment. However, the incidence of cancers has risen among the local population. Recent computer models predict radioactive material buried at Mururoa will leak to the sea within decades.

Opposition to nuclear testing in Oceania has been led by the environmental group 'Greenpeace'. In 1985, French secret agents bombed the Greenpeace ship, *Rainbow Warrior*, in Auckland harbour in New Zealand, and killed one of the crew. In 1995, Greenpeace continued to actively oppose the French testing.

FOREIGN AID

The future development of some nations in Oceania depends on foreign financial aid. Australia and New Zealand are the major sources of regional assistance. Australia spends 20 per cent of its foreign aid budget on Papua New Guinea alone. About 70 per cent of New Zealand's foreign aid is distributed in Oceania. France and the USA continue to provide aid to islands under their administration. Aid programmes enable the nations of Oceania to buy imports, build schools and hospitals, and fund new techniques in agriculture and industry that will lead to greater self-sufficiency.

Nuclear testing by France in 1995 resulted in widespread anger in Australia and Oceania. In Paris, French citizens demonstrated against their own government.

Pour le «rayonnement» de la France, merci Chirac !

Pour la prolifération nucléaire, merci Chirac

AUSTRALIA AND OCEANIA IN THE WORLD TODAY

Modern communications technology means that Australia and Oceania are no longer isolated from the rest of the world. Their economic development is closely related to trends in the world economy, and their attempts to solve environmental problems must be seen as a world concern. At the same time, a new sense of regional identity is emerging in the Pacific. In particular, Australia is becoming more influential in the economic and cultural affairs of the Asia-Pacific area.

TOURISM

Since the 1960s, tourism has become an important source of income in Oceania. Tourism has stimulated the building of roads, airports, shops, luxury hotels and restaurants. It has provided employment for local people, although mainly in the services sector. Some tourist resorts, however, are foreign-owned and bring little economic benefit to local populations. The Cook Islands, Vanuatu, Fiji, American Samoa, Western Samoa, Guam and Tahiti in French Polynesia encourage tourism. Other islands are wary of the impact of visitors on their environment and culture.

Tourism to Australia increased during the 1980s and the industry now employs 6 per cent of the workforce. One of the challenges in Australia and Oceania is to maintain 'environmentally friendly' tourism, but it seems certain that tourism will play a significant role in the economic future of the region.

The Pacific 'paradise' of tropical beaches and spectacular scenery, friendly lifestyles and 'exotic' cultures is promoted by tourist agencies around the world. Tourism depends on people having spare money to spend on holidays, so it can be vulnerable to changes in the world's economy.

REGIONAL COOPERATION IN OCEANIA

Most nations in Oceania are too small to have any significant role in international matters, so they have united into organizations centred around their region to strengthen their voice. There are more than 200 regional organizations in Oceania today, linking the nations' interests in the fields of government, education, business and the arts.

In 1947, the South Pacific Commission was established by Australia, France, Britain, New Zealand and the USA to promote development in Oceania. In 1971, the more influential South Pacific Forum was set up by the independent nations in the region, including Australia. The Forum meets each year to discuss trade, communications, shipping, the environment, fishing laws and political issues. The Regional Trade and Economic Cooperation Agreement helps trade between Australia, New Zealand and the nations of Oceania.

Since 1989, the Asia-Pacific Economic Cooperation Forum (APEC) has encouraged cooperation with the wider Asia-Pacific region. Australia and New Zealand are associate members of the Association of Southeast Asian Nations (ASEAN). These regional organizations and agreements will have an important effect on the economic and social development of Australia and Oceania in the twenty-first century.

Above Two of Sydney's older architectural features, the Harbour Bridge and the Opera House (shown here), are recognized internationally as symbols of Australia.

Below More than 3 million foreign visitors arrive in Australia each year. These figures will rise substantially when the Olympic Games are held in Sydney, in the year 2000.

TIMELINE

BC c.50,000 Human settlement of Australia and New Guinea.

c.12,000 Island of Tasmania separates from Australia.

c 8,000 New Guinea separated from Australian mainland.

c.2,000 Sea-faring peoples from Southeast Asia begin to arrive in parts of Melanesia, and from there travel to, and settle in, Micronesia and Polynesia.

AD c.400-1600 Stone sculptures are erected in Easter Island.

c.1300 Maori settlement in New Zealand. The Maori developed a complex society with unique rituals and culture. The land was fertile enough for them to have free time from farming activities, and their society was based on war-like clans which lived in fortified hilltop villages called *pa*. From these *pa*, warriors with tattooed faces set out to do battle with the members of other tribes.

1513 Spanish explorer Vasco Nunez de Balboa becomes the first European to sight the Pacific Ocean.

1500s-1700s European exploration and mapping of the Pacific. Spanish, Portuguese, Dutch and English explorers, among others, spread through Oceania in search of spices and the mythical wealth of the region, hoping to return to Europe as rich men.

1565 Guam claimed by Spain.

1769-70 Captain James Cook explores the coastline of New Zealand.

1770 Captain James Cook claims eastern half of Australia as British possession.

1788 First fleet of convicts arrives in Sydney, Australia. Most of the first sailors in Australia were convicts, soldiers or government officials. Transportation to Australia was a common punishment for criminals in the eighteenth and nineteenth centuries in Britain.

1790 The *Bounty* mutineers led by Fletcher Christian settle on Pitcairn Island.

1830 Britain has claimed the entire continent of Australia as a colonial possession by this time. The numbers of free settlers, as opposed to convicts, begins to increase from this point onwards.

1840 Treaty of Waitangi is signed between Maori and British; New Zealand becomes a British colony.

1842 French Polynesia and Tahiti become French protectorates.

1850s Gold discovered in Australia, bringing thousands of European settlers.

1853 Britain grants New Zealand the right to form representative institutions.

1860 Gold discovered in New Zealand.

1860-70 War in New Zealand between British and Maori over ownership of land. The Land Wars end with British victory in 1870.

1874 Fiji proclaimed a British colony.

1875 Tonga adopts a constitutional monarchy.

1879-1920 Labourers from India are brought to Fiji. Most are contract labourers, who are paid a fixed amount for a fixed number of years' service. Many never returned to India, instead buying land in Fiji and settling there. Conflict between these immigrants and the native Fijians, who were the land's original occupants, continues today.

1888 Britain assumes control of the Cook Islands. Easter Island annexed by Chile.

1899 USA takes Guam from Spain.

1900 Tonga becomes a British protectorate.

1901 Federation of Australian colonies become one nation.

1901 Cook Islands controlled by New Zealand.

1921 German New Guinea under Australian control.

1941-45 The Second World War is fought in parts of Oceania.

1946 French Polynesia granted overseas territory status by France, with limited self-government.

1947 UN Trust Territory of the Pacific Islands, administered by the USA, formed.

1947 South Pacific Commission established by Australia, France, Britain, New Zealand, and USA to promote economic development in Oceania.

1950s-60s British atomic tests in Australia and Polynesia; USA atomic tests in Micronesia; French atomic tests in Polynesia.

1962 Western Samoa gains independence.

1965 Cook Islands granted self-government.

1968 Nauru gains independence.

1970 Tonga gains independence; Fiji gains independence.

1973 Australia abandons immigration policies that favour European – especially British – immigrants, as Britain joins the European Community. From this point on, Australia starts to reorientate itself towards the other Pacific nations.

1975 Papua New Guinea gains independence.

1978 Tuvalu gains independence. Northern Mariana Islands become self-governing under US control.

1979 Kiribati gains independence.

1980 Vanuatu gains independence.

1985 French secret agents bomb Greenpeace ship, Rainbow Warrior, in Auckland, New Zealand.

1986 The UN Trust Territory of the Pacific Islands is dissolved. Of the four political districts that made it up: the Republic of the Marshall Islands and the Federated States of Micronesia entered into a free association agreement with the USA; the Commonwealth of the Northern Mariana Islands became a commonwealth of the USA; and Palau remained in the trusteeship of the USA.

1987 Two military coups in Fiji, both led by Lieutentant-Colonel Rabuka, an ethnic Fijian. The coups take place against a background of tension between ethnic Fijians and the descendants of Indian immigrants. After the second coup, Fiji is expelled from the British Commonwealth, and becomes a republic.

1993 Native Title Bill passed in Australia, recognizing Aboriginal ownership of land prior to British settlement.

1995 In New Zealand, Waikato Taupatu Claims Bill signed by Queen Elizabeth II

1995 French atomic testing in French Polynesia. France continues its tests despite protests from all neighbouring Pacific nations and international organizations. Greenpeace attempts to disrupt the tests are not effective.

GLOSSARY

Aborgine Aborigines are the indigenous peoples of Australia.

Admistration How a country is run.

Alpine Climatic conditions in a cool, mountainous region.

Arable Farming where crops are grown.

Archipelago A group or cluster of islands.

Arid Dry (land or climate) with an annual rainfall of less than 250 mm.

Atmospheric pressure The level of air pressure in the atmosphere.

Atoll A coral island, where a ring-shaped coral reef encloses a lagoon.

Atomic bomb A bomb that derives its power from atomic energy.

Cash crops Crops grown specifically for export to generate income for a country.

Culture Aspects of a country or society that make it distinctive – its way of life, art, music, religion.

Cyclone Very strong winds that rotate around a small area with the ability to cause great damage.

Ecosystem The interaction between a living community and its environment.

Evolve To develop over time.

Exports Agricultural and manufactured products that are sent out of the country to another country as traded goods.

Extinct A species that has died out.

Foreign debt How much a country owes other countries or international banks.

Foreign investment Foreign money, or money of another country, invested or used for business.

Germinate To begin to develop and grow.

Indigenous Native to a particular geographical area.

Manufacturing Products that are made through manual labour, such as basket weaving, and machinery, such as woollen jumpers or motor cars.

Multiculturalism Policy of acceptance of many different cultures.

Native title The legal recognition that Aboriginal people have traditional land rights.

Ochre A pigment used to make yellow or red paint.

Oscillation Changes or variations.

Plateau A large area of flat land.

Regeneration Growing again, renewing.

Saltpan Low-lying area where water evaporation has left a salt residue.

Sanitation Conditions of dirt and infection that affect health.

Self-sufficiency Producing enough to fulfill one's own needs.

Service industry Work that serves customers directly, such as a shop assistant or hotel worker.

Shanty-towns Poorly constructed housing, usually without amenities like running water or sewerage.

Subsistence When people grow crops to support themselves rather than selling for profit.

Sustainable development Growth that can be maintained.

Temperate A moderate or mild climate.

Tropical Hot and humid climatic conditions.

Tuber plants Plant with fleshy roots.

Urbanized Where a large proportion of the population is concentrated in towns and cities.

Vocational Related to employment, or to professional careers.

FURTHER INFORMATION

Non-fiction for children
Australia (Country Fact Files series), Macdonald Young Books, 1996.
Australia (Modern Industrial World series) by Lowe and Darian-Smith, Wayland, 1995.
Australian Aborigines (Threatened Cultures series) by Richard Nile, Wayland, 1993.
The Australian Outback and Its People (People and Places series) by Lowe and Darian-Smith, Wayland, 1993.
The Pacific Ocean (Seas and Oceans series) by David Lambert, Wayland, 1996.

Reference/non-fiction material
Chronicle of the Twentieth Century, J L International Publications, 1994.
Collins Atlas of World History, Collins, 1987.
Exploration into Australia by Darian-Smith, Kate, Belitha Press/Royal Geographical Society, London, 1995.
The Economist Book of Vital World Statistics, The Economist (latest edition).
The Economist World Atlas, The Economist, 1992.
The Guinness Guide to People and Cultures, Guinness Publishing, 1992.
Philips Encyclopaedic World Atlas, George Philips, 1993.
Philips Geographical Digest 1996–97, Heinemann Educational, 1996.
Times Atlas of World History, Times Publishers, 1993.

Atlases published after 1993 are a useful source of information; so are modern encyclopaedias, especially those on CD-Rom.

Films
Australia and New Zealand both have sizeable film industries.
The Piano, which should be in your local video shop, is about a young girl whose mother travels to New Zealand in the nineteenth century to get married. It's a film for adults, so you must check with an adult before watching it.
Proof is an Australian film about a blind photographer.
Once Were Warriors is about modern life among the Maori of New Zealand's cities. Again, you must check with an adult before watching this film.

INDEX

919

**Books are to be returned on or before
the last date below**

2 2 JUN 1999	2 0 AUG 2008	
2 3 JUN 1999		
- 1 NOV 1999	1 8 MAY 2011	
1 0 JAN 2000	1 6 APR 2012	
1 2 JAN 2000	2 3 SEP 2014	
1 9 APR 2000	2 4 NOV 2014	
1 6 APR 2002		
2 4 JUN 2002		
2 1 AUG 2002		
2 1 AUG 2002		
2 2 APR 2004		
- 7 APR 2008		
0 3 JUN 2008		
2 0 AUG 2008		

LIBREX —